ALL–STAR SMACK>> DOWN

LEBRON JAMES VS. MICHAEL JORDAN

WHO WOULD WIN?

KEITH ELLIOT GREENBERG

Lerner Publications ◆ Minneapolis

SPORTS THRILLS MEET RESEARCH SKILLS

Lerner SPORTS

Free Database Trial: **lernersports.com**

Lerner Publications Company
An imprint of Lerner Publishing Group, Inc.
241 First Avenue North
Minneapolis, MN 55401 USA

For reading levels and more information, look up this title at www.lernerbooks.com.

Main body text set in Aptifer Sans LT Pro.
Typeface provided by Linotype AG.

Library of Congress Cataloging-in-Publication Data

Names: Greenberg, Keith Elliot, 1959– author.
Title: LeBron James vs. Michael Jordan: who would win? / Keith Elliot Greenberg.
Other titles: LeBron James versus Michael Jordan
Description: Minneapolis, MN: Lerner Publications, [2024] | Series: Lerner sports. All-star smackdown | Includes bibliographical references and index. | Audience: Ages 7–11 | Audience: Grades 2–3 | Summary: "Michael Jordan and LeBron James have both led the NBA in points and game wins. But who is the best player of all time? Compare their achievements and careers to find out for yourself"— Provided by publisher.
Identifiers: LCCN 2022044310 (print) | LCCN 2022044311 (ebook) | ISBN 9781728490878 (library binding) | ISBN 9798765602454 (paperback) | ISBN 9781728495743 (ebook)
Subjects: LCSH: James, LeBron—Juvenile literature. | Jordan, Michael, 1963– —Juvenile literature. | Basketball players—United States—Biography—Juvenile literature.
Classification: LCC GV884.J36 G73 2024 (print) | LCC GV884.J36 (ebook) | DDC 796.323092 [B]—dc23/eng/20220930

LC record available at https://lccn.loc.gov/2022044310
LC ebook record available at https://lccn.loc.gov/2022044311

Manufactured in the United States of America
4-1010356-51036-11/6/2023

TABLE OF CONTENTS

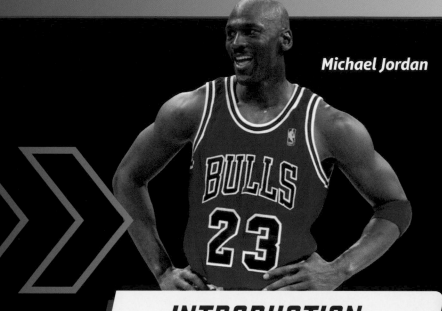

Michael Jordan

INTRODUCTION

TWO BASKETBALL GREATS

It was the sixth game of the 1998 National Basketball Association (NBA) Finals. The Chicago Bulls had won three games in the seven-match series. But Chicago trailed the Utah Jazz near the end of Game 6. That's when Michael Jordan took over.

 FAST FACTS

- ✪ Michael Jordan won five NBA Most Valuable Player (MVP) awards.

- ✪ Jordan was an NBA Finals MVP six times.

- ✪ LeBron James was the first player to score at least 10 points in 1,000 NBA games in a row.

- ✪ James has won the NBA championship with three different teams.

Jordan beat the Jazz defense and scored, tying the game 85–85. As Utah tried to score, Jordan took the ball from them. With five seconds left, he scored a jump shot. The Bulls were the series champions and Jordan was the NBA Finals MVP.

Eighteen years later, LeBron James led the Cleveland Cavaliers to victory and became a new basketball hero. Game 7 of the 2016 NBA Finals between the Cavaliers and the Golden State Warriors would decide the champion. The score was tied with less than two minutes left.

LeBron James

Warriors player Andre Iguodala grabbed the ball. He went for a close shot, but James leaped and blocked the ball. In the game's final seconds, James scored from the free throw line to give Cleveland a four-point lead. For the first time, the Cavaliers were NBA champions. James had more points, rebounds, and blocks than any other player in the series. He won the Finals MVP award.

Jordan was known for his ability to leap high in the air, so his nickname was Air Jordan. James's nicknames include King James and the Chosen One. With his large size, he can push his way past defenders to score or pass the ball to open teammates.

Which player is better? That's up to you to decide. Let the smackdown begin!

Michael Jordan drives for the score during the 1998 NBA playoffs.

LeBron James jumps for an easy basket against Stephen Curry and the Warriors during the 2016 NBA Finals.

CHAPTER 1

Left to right: *Michael Jordan, Deloris Jordan, and James Jordan eat a cake shaped like a Nike Air Jordan shoe.*

THE ROAD TO THE NBA

Michael Jordan was born in 1963 in Brooklyn, New York. His mother, Deloris, worked in a bank. His father, James, was an equipment supervisor. When Michael was five years old, the family moved to Wilmington, North Carolina.

Both Michael and his father loved baseball. Michael's older brother, Larry, was a great basketball player. Since Michael looked up to Larry, he decided to try playing basketball too.

During his sophomore year at Emsley A. Laney High School, Michael was too short to play for the varsity team. He had grown by the time his junior year started. Michael joined the varsity team and averaged more than 25 points per game.

The gym at Emsley A. Laney High School in Wilmington is named after former student Michael Jordan.

Jordan takes a shot in a college game against Indiana in 1984.

Jordan dribbles with his tongue sticking out of his mouth. He often stuck out his tongue during Bulls games.

When he graduated, Jordan accepted a scholarship to play for the University of North Carolina at Chapel Hill. In 1982, he played in the college championship game against Georgetown University. Georgetown was led by future NBA player Patrick Ewing. With millions of basketball fans watching, Jordan scored the winning shot.

He left college after his junior year to enter the 1984 NBA Draft. The Bulls chose him as the third overall pick. In his first season, he was both an All-Star and the NBA Rookie of the Year. He was so popular in the NBA that fans of other teams cheered for him.

LeBron James was born in 1984 in Akron, Ohio. LeBron's mother, Gloria, wanted her son to have a good future and believed sports would help him. Local football coach Frank Walter invited the nine-year-old boy to live with him. Gloria agreed. Walter introduced LeBron to basketball.

LeBron was such a good basketball player that a private high school, St. Vincent-St. Mary, asked him to play for them. LeBron was one of the few Black students at the school. He played so well that thousands of people came to see his games. The school began playing in a larger arena at the University of Akron.

Many fans think James was the greatest player in high school basketball history.

James soars for a slam dunk in 2003.

FOX8

THINK FOX FIRST

Although he was just a teenager, many people thought LeBron was good enough to play in the NBA. His favorite team, the Cleveland Cavaliers, selected him as the first overall pick in the 2003 NBA Draft. He chose to wear number 23 on his jersey. He wanted the same number that his hero Michael Jordan had worn.

Like Jordan, James was the NBA Rookie of the Year in his first season. No other Cavaliers player had ever won that honor. Many more honors and awards lay ahead for James.

LeBron James with NBA commissioner David Stern at the 2003 NBA Draft

James averaged 27.2 points per game for the Cavaliers in 2004–2005. He led the team in scoring by more than ten points per game.

CHAPTER 2

Michael Jordan passes the ball in Game 5 of the 1997 NBA Finals.

GREATEST MOMENTS

During a memorable game in 1997, Michael Jordan proved he was a warrior on the court. The Chicago Bulls were playing in Game 5 of the NBA Finals against the Utah Jazz. The series was tied 2–2. Jordan had a stomach illness and a fever. But he played anyway.

The Jazz were thrilled to take an early 16-point lead. But in the second quarter, Jordan jumped into action and scored 17 points. In the fourth quarter, he scored 15 points. With

25 seconds left in the game, he made a long three-point shot. After the Bulls won 90–88, Jordan was worn out. Teammate Scottie Pippen helped him leave the court.

Fans call the game against Utah the Flu Game because Jordan was sick. It was one of Jordan's many special moments in the NBA. Others include a 1990 game when he scored an amazing 69 points. He also made the winning shot in the last game of the 1998 NBA Finals.

LeBron James quickly became a team leader with the Cavaliers and began racking up his own amazing moments.

Scottie Pippen (right) helps Jordan off the court after the Bulls won the Flu Game during the 1997 NBA Finals.

During the 2009–2010 season, he made the job look easy. The Cavaliers had the best record in the NBA. But they lost in the second round of the playoffs.

After the season, James was free to join any team in the NBA. He decided to go to the Miami Heat. James returned to

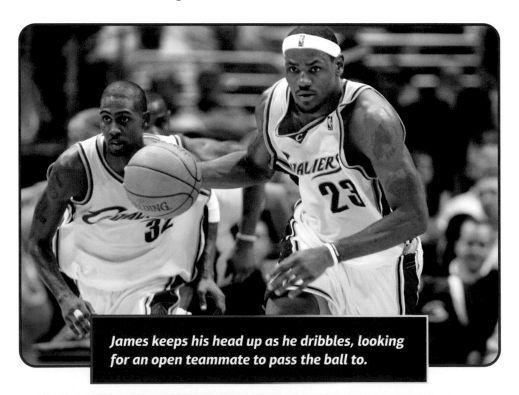

James keeps his head up as he dribbles, looking for an open teammate to pass the ball to.

James won the NBA MVP award for the third time in his second season with the Miami Heat.

Cleveland with the Heat in 2010–2011 to play against his old team, and Cavaliers fans booed him. But he still scored 38 points in the game.

In the 2011 playoffs against the Boston Celtics, James scored the final 10 points in Game 5 to win the series. He knelt on the court to let his Miami fans know how much they meant to him. The next year, he scored 61 points in a game against the Charlotte Bobcats. It was the most points he had ever scored in a single game in his career.

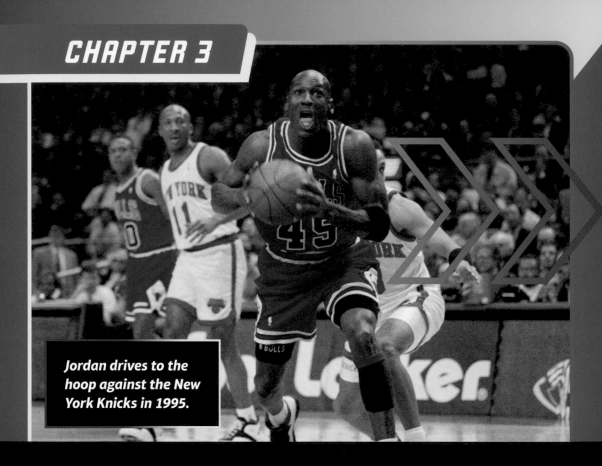

CHAPTER 3

Jordan drives to the hoop against the New York Knicks in 1995.

TAKING HOME THE TROPHY

For many basketball fans, the first name that comes to mind when thinking of NBA champions is Michael Jordan. Throughout his career, his NBA Finals series record was perfect. He won the championship series six times and never lost it.

Jordan's father died suddenly in 1993. After the death, Jordan left the NBA for two years. During that time, he played minor league baseball for the Birmingham Barons.

In 1995–1996, Jordan was back with the Bulls. That season, Game 6 of the NBA Finals took place on Father's Day. Jordan led the Bulls to the series victory against the Seattle SuperSonics. After the game, Jordan held the ball and cried.

Jordan (right) hugs teammate Randy Brown near the end of Game 6 of the 1996 NBA Finals.

LeBron James played in the NBA Finals every season from 2011 to 2018. He won his first two NBA championships as a member of the Miami Heat in 2012 and 2013. But in 2014, he decided to return to the Cleveland Cavaliers. The fans who had booed him when he left for Miami cheered him on again. They knew his goal was the same as theirs. They wanted to bring the NBA championship trophy to Cleveland.

When he helped the Cavaliers win the prize in 2016, James was thrilled. After the final buzzer sounded, he cried and told Cleveland fans that the championship was for them. Around the city, people celebrated.

James left Cleveland after the 2017–2018 season and joined the Los Angeles Lakers. He led his new team to the 2020 NBA Finals. When the Lakers beat the Heat in the Finals, James became only the fourth player to win the NBA championship with three different teams.

James dunks the ball in a game against the Philadelphia 76ers in 2020.

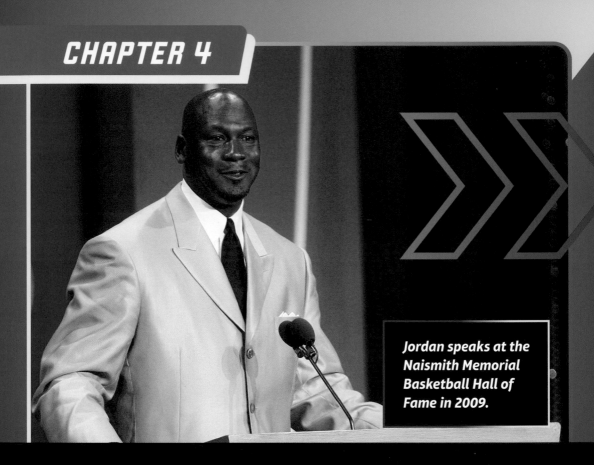

CHAPTER 4

Jordan speaks at the Naismith Memorial Basketball Hall of Fame in 2009.

AND THE WINNER IS

In this NBA All-Star smackdown, who comes out on top? You can decide for yourself. For years, people have debated which superstar is the best of all time. It's part of the fun of being a basketball fan!

Michael Jordan retired after the 1997–1998 season. But he returned to the NBA in 2001–2002 and became a co-owner of the Washington Wizards. He also joined the team as a player and donated some of the money he earned to charity.

His passion for the game and its fans made basketball more popular all over the world.

Jordan joined the Naismith Memorial Basketball Hall of Fame in 2009. LeBron James is certain to become a Hall of Famer soon after he retires. James has been an NBA All-Star 19 times compared to Jordan's 14. Yet James has been helped by playing with many great teammates. Some fans

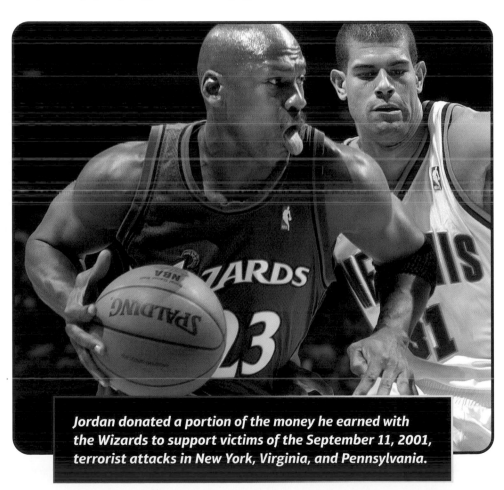

Jordan donated a portion of the money he earned with the Wizards to support victims of the September 11, 2001, terrorist attacks in New York, Virginia, and Pennsylvania.

say Jordan was more important to his team because his teammates weren't as good as James's.

In 2020, James became the first NBA player to score 10 points or more in 1,000 straight games. Two years later, he became the only player with 10,000 points, 10,000 rebounds, and 10,000 assists. In 2023, James passed Kareem Abdul-Jabbar to become the NBA's all-time scoring leader.

For more than 20 seasons, James has been a leader for his teams and the league. He is the NBA's greatest scorer and the winner of this smackdown. Who do you think the winner is? Look at the stats, then make your own choice!

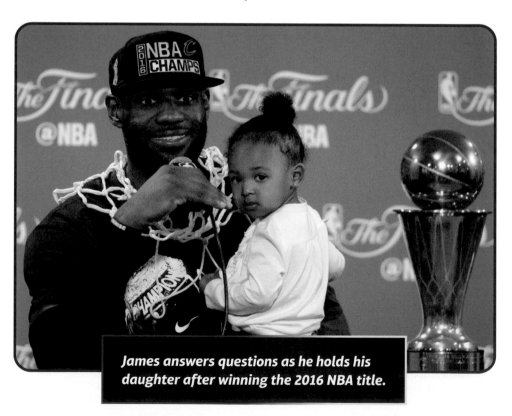

James answers questions as he holds his daughter after winning the 2016 NBA title.

With every basket James scores, he adds to his all-time NBA scoring record.

MICHAEL JORDAN

Date of birth: February 17, 1963
Height: 6 feet 6 (1.9 m)
NBA championships: 6
NBA MVP awards: 5
NBA All-Star Games: 14
Olympic gold medals: 2

LEBRON JAMES

Date of birth: December 30, 1984
Height: 6 feet 9 (2.1 m)
NBA championships: 4
NBA MVP awards: 4
NBA All-Star Games: 19
Olympic gold medals: 2

GLOSSARY

assist: a pass from a teammate that leads directly to a score

draft: when teams take turns choosing new players

free throw: an open shot taken from behind a line on the court after a foul by an opponent

jump shot: a shot made by jumping into the air while releasing the ball with one or both hands

minor league: a professional baseball league below the Major Leagues

rebound: when a player grabs a missed shot

rookie: a first-year player

scholarship: money a student receives to help pay for school

varsity: the top team at a school

LEARN MORE

Aretha, David. *LeBron vs. Durant vs. Curry vs. Jordan*. New York: Rosen, 2020.

Basketball Facts for Kids
https://kids.kiddle.co/Basketball

LeBron James Official Website
https://www.lebronjames.com/

Levit, Joe. *Michael Jordan: Flying High*. Minneapolis: Lerner Publications, 2021.

Michael Jordan Facts for Kids
https://www.factsjustforkids.com/famous-people-facts/michael-jordan-facts-for-kids/

Wetzel, Dan. *Epic Athletes: LeBron James*. New York: Henry Holt and Company, 2019.

INDEX

PHOTO ACKNOWLEDGMENTS

Image credits: AP Photo/Alan Mothner, p. 4; Ed Suba Jr./Akron Beacon Journal/MCT/Cameleon/ABACAPRESS.COM/Alamy Stock Photo, p. 5; AP Photo/Mike Fisher, p. 6; Carlos Avila Gonzalez/San Francisco Chronicle/Getty Images, p. 7; AP Photo/Charles Bennett, p. 8; Edward Orde/Wikipedia Commons, p. 9; PCN Photography/Alamy Stock Photo, p. 10; Focus on Sport/agency/Getty Images, p.11; AP Photo/Tony Dejak, p. 12; AP Photo/Bruce Schwartzman, p. 13; AP Photo/Ed Betz, p.14; Mike Kepka/San Francisco Chronicle/Getty Images, p. 15; AP Photo/Jack Smith, pp. 16, 17; AP Photo/Mark Duncan, p. 18; Mike Ehrmann/Getty Images, p. 19; AP Photo/Kevin Larkin, p. 20; AP Photo/Michael Conroy, p.21; Katelyn Mulcahy/Getty Images, p. 23; Jim Rogash/Getty Images, p. 24; AP Photo/Nikki Boertman, p. 25; AP Photo/Eric Risberg, p. 26; Steph Chambers/Getty Images, p. 27; AP Photo/Al Messerschmidt, p. 28; GEORGE FREY/AFP/Getty Images, p. 29.

Cover: AP Photo/Tom DiPace, (Michael Jordan); AP Photo/Jae C. Hong (Lebron James).